JUST BEST FRIENDS

(Recollections of a Golden Retriever)

Trafford
PUBLISHING™

Order this book online at www.trafford.com
or email orders@trafford.com

Most Trafford titles are also available at major online book retailers.

© Copyright 2009 Guy Winch.
All rights reserved. No part of this publication may be reproduced, stored in a retrieval
system, or transmitted, in any form or by any means, electronic, mechanical, photocopying,
recording, or otherwise, without the written prior permission of the author.

Note for Librarians: A cataloguing record for this book is available from Library
and Archives Canada at www.collectionscanada.ca/amicus/index-e.html

Printed in Victoria, BC, Canada.

ISBN: 978-1-4251-8866-5 (sc)

*We at Trafford believe that it is the responsibility of us all, as both individuals
and corporations, to make choices that are environmentally and socially sound.
You, in turn, are supporting this responsible conduct each time you purchase a
Trafford book, or make use of our publishing services. To find out how you are
helping, please visit www.trafford.com/responsiblepublishing.html*

*Our mission is to efficiently provide the world's finest, most comprehensive
book publishing service, enabling every author to experience success.
To find out how to publish your book, your way, and have it available
worldwide, visit us online at www.trafford.com*

Trafford rev. 5/26/2009

20% of all net proceeds from the sale of this book will be donated to the SPCA.

 www.trafford.com

North America & international
toll-free: 1 888 232 4444 (USA & Canada)
phone: 250 383 6864 ♦ fax: 250 383 6804 ♦ email: info@trafford.com

The United Kingdom & Europe
phone: +44 (0)1865 487 395 ♦ local rate: 0845 230 9601
facsimile: +44 (0)1865 481 507 ♦ email: info.uk@trafford.com

10 9 8 7 6 5 4 3 2

CHAPTER I

Generally speaking there are two kinds of people in this world; those that like dogs... and those that don't. And if you're a dog, it doesn't take much to sort one out from the other.

As everyone knows, we have a very highly developed olfactory system. (That's a superior sort of way of saying we have a sensitive nose). But what I'll bet you don't know is, that the people who don't like us, have a special sort of smell. It's a curious, mouldy, sour sort of smell really, which I suppose, in a way, reflects their personality. It's not actually their fault. It's just the way they are. Anyway, what with the scent, plus all the body language that goes along with it, it doesn't take much to sniff them out. They don't like us, and to tell you the truth, we're not too fussy about them, so I guess it's mutual.

So, should you happen to belong to the latter category, (I mean if you're a 'non-dog- liker'), then read no further, for this book is not for you... Unless of course you'd like to read about my early sexual exploits. They appear on page twenty- three.

I put that in because my master says that nowadays a book won't sell, and simply has no public appeal without some explicit juicy sex bits. It's true. People just seem to be obsessed with sex, don't they? Did you know that the Psychologists, after an in depth study, have found that the average person spends at least one hour of every waking day, thinking about sex? And that's not even mentioning what goes on at night!

Talking about books. My master says that whenever you borrow a book, almost invariably, it seems to automatically fall open at these illuminating pages. These always seem to be a bit more tattered and well thumbed than the other pages, and if you look closely, you'll find a small crease at the corner, where it has been bent over to serve as a bookmark for easier and more immediate access. He says it's very bad form to do this, as it shows disrespect for the writer.

For me, sex has always been a most wholesome and pleasurable pastime, but there are, after all, other things in life, which especially for a dog, are just as important...well, almost.

But then you already know all that.

So... now that you have quite finished devouring page twenty-three, perhaps we could begin.

Ready?

I have always wanted to tell my story, but because I am who I am, there are those who might think that I don't qualify, because I was never really what you might call a celebrity. But memoirs are after all memoirs; recollections are important. Besides as one gets older it has become the fashionable thing to do, (at least that's what my boss says). Anyone who is anybody is doing it, and I have just as much right to go down in posterity as any one else, so let me tell my story and you be the judge.

To begin with, although it causes me some embarrassment, and because I am well aware that well bred people should never really talk about themselves in this way, but I do actually come from a long lineage of a rather distinguished and aristocratic family, which of course most people who are aware of such matters, would recognize immediately from my profile.

My grandfather happened to have been the North of England champion in his day, and my father, who was one of several offspring, was actually shipped over to Canada when he was quite young. He too grew up to be quite famous, and won several awards. He was much sought after by the ladies for he was very good looking, and they all chased after him, hoping to become part of our distinguished background, and to bask in the glory, and share in the glittering prizes to be won.

I am really not entirely sure as to how my mother and father met, but I believe it was in a place called Merritt. I can't imagine

4

what a distinguished personage such as my father was doing in such a small town, but he certainly did not tarry there for long. I am sorry to say I never really knew him, for some months before I was born, he had to leave my mother and return to Vancouver. All rather sad, but then that's the way it is sometimes.

My mother of course was a renowned beauty, and was known not just for her looks, but for her soft and gentle nature. She was very special and I adored her.

I don't remember much about those early days and first few weeks after I was born, but I do recall that I had two sisters and four brothers, all of whom were my age, and with whom I used to romp and play, under the watchful eye of our mother.

I was about eight weeks old when disaster struck.

The lady of the house in which we were all living, came into our play area one day, accompanied by a nice looking middle aged man, who obviously liked us, and was most friendly. He smelled of dogs and horse manure. He and the lady of the house seemed to be engaged in a very serious conversation. We were of course far too young to understand what it was about, but our mum did. She had been there before, and she knew exactly what was going to happen. Obviously it was serious, because she suddenly became very agitated; we had never seen her look so distraught or sad.

After a while the kindly middle aged man nodded to the lady, and they went back into the house together.

It was then that our mum talked to us, and explained what was going to happen. Oh God! We were going to be taken away! We couldn't believe that we were going to be separated from our mum.

She was wonderful. She explained to us very calmly that Mrs Smithers (the lady whose house we lived in), loved us all very much, but that she could not afford to keep us all for ever, and that the nice man who had come to see us, was going to take us away to a place near Vancouver called Langley, where he had a big farm, where he kept a school for people like us which was called a kennel, and that we were to stay there for a while, where we would be well looked after, until he was able to find a suitable home for each one of us.

Well, this was a terrible blow, but our mum talked to us in her own special way. She explained to us who we really were, and what our role in life was meant to be. It had to do with being loving and loyal and protective, and being part of a family.

She said: 'You must remember that you are really people dogs, but never forget that you are also GOLDEN RETRIEVERS and are very special. You have a reputation to live up to.'

My sisters began to whimper and cry, while my brothers and I huddled together next to our mum. We didn't feel like playing anymore. It was a bad scene, and one that I would rather forget.

In a short while, the nice man returned with a big box lined with straw, which was placed in the back of his van. My mum licked each one of us goodbye as we were taken away. It was awful, and we all started to cry.

We had never been in a car before. It was noisy, and all the more scary because there were no windows, we couldn't see out, and we had no idea as to where we were going or how long it would take, and the motion of the car going around corners was making us feel a bit sick. After what seemed a very long time we finally arrived at Langley. The nice man, whose name we discovered was Jack, opened the door and we all jumped out.

Much to our surprise, we were greeted by welcoming barks from a whole lot of other dogs of all ages, who were attending the school there. We were of course by far the youngest, so we had to be quite respectful, especially to the most senior, who was also a Golden Retriever. He was known as 'Major'. You could tell that he had been around for quite a while by the gray hairs around his snout, and he had a definite air of authority which clearly announced 'don't mess with me'. He was an expert retriever, he knew how to count in numbers, and exactly which decoy to fetch when told, and Jack used him to help train the other dogs. He was very much aware of how important he was, and we all thought that Major was a pretty good name for him.

He had what we figured must have been a girl friend; she was also a golden retriever, and her name was Casey. Like our mum, she was very gentle, and she took it upon herself to watch over us, and keep us from getting into too much mischief, and getting into trouble with the other dogs. Anyway, she and Major always slept together in their own little house, and between the two of them, and of course Jack, they pretty well ran the place. It was said that Casey and Major had had quite a number of puppies together, some of whom had grown up to be champion retrievers and won all sorts of prizes. No wonder Major was so proud!

For myself, I wasn't all that crazy about this retrieving business. I thought it was much more fun to have someone chase after me to retrieve the 'bird', which of course wasn't a bird at all, but just a bag filled with straw, which was just the thing to put one's teeth into and tear it apart. I got into real big trouble from Major for this, and got a proper telling off I can tell you. He told me I was a disgrace to my ancestry, and that I would grow up to be a useless hound, and a whole lot more. I had never heard such language! To tell you the truth I didn't really mind all that much, for as I said, I wasn't exactly aiming to be a champion bird dog; I hated the noise made by that gun thing they used to kill the poor birds, and I had already decided that all I really wanted out of life was to be what they called a family pooch. But in the right kind of family of course.

Two or three weeks went by, and during this time we were given a bit more schooling. Not just in bird dogging, (in which they had pretty well given up with me), but in other ways, as how to behave, such as how to sit and stay, to lie down, and of course where and when to poop. I don't know why this is so often referred to as 'doing one's business'. Perhaps some people have an aversion to the word poop, but I always thought that this was a much more satisfactory and descriptive way of describing something which is a very personal thing, which I prefer to do in private, and do not like being watched when I do it. After all would you? We are all entitled to a bit of privacy, don't you think?

Anyway as time passed, there were some other developments that occurred that we watched very carefully. Every few days or so, we would have people come to visit and inspect us. This was always preceded by being washed and brushed, that was a job usually given to Jack's son Derwent. (Funny name that isn't it?), but then his mother was Irish, so perhaps that explains it. Derwent was only sixteen, and used to play with us quite a bit and was really nice. He used to help his mum and dad with the chores around the farm, and became very popular with us, because he brought us our food.

But to get back to this inspection business. Sometimes it was just one person that came, usually a man, but sometimes a lady. They would look at us in a very professional way, but never showed us much affection. We sort of got the impression that we were being looked at more for commercial value, much like horse flesh, and were being considered more for our breeding potential than anything else. And while there is certainly nothing wrong with breeding, either from a theoretical, and even more importantly, from a practical point of view, I did not like their attitude. I got poor vibes from them.

So when it came to my turn to be inspected, I declined to stand properly. And rather than assuming the 'point position', I'd keep all four feet firmly on the ground, and let my tail go all droopy, and at the same time put on my dumbest and most unintelligent expression. I would pretend that I had no idea how to sit, and didn't even understand 'come'. Poor Jack would get quite embarrassed, but I was determined that I was going to go to the right home and to the right family.

On two occasions a family of two or three came. They really liked us. You could tell by the way they petted and stroked us, and they had the right smells. On each of these occasions we had to say goodbye to one of our brothers or sisters, which was of course very sad for us, but we were comforted by knowing that they were going to a good home and that they would be happy there.

I knew that if I was patient and played my cards right, that my turn would surely come. There were just the three of us left, when about two weeks later it happened. Jack had heard that they were coming, so we had had the usual bath and brush routine, and were of course looking our most beautiful best. Well, I thought so anyway. I just had a feeling that it might be my day.

The family arrived in a big blue car, and I knew right from the start that they were going to be alright. There were seven people, a man, his wife, and five girls, and the man was telling the kids: "Now don't get all excited, we are just going to look at the puppies, we are not necessarily going to take one home"- but of course I knew better, because I had already summed up the situation, and could see that both the man and his wife were an absolute pushover as far as dogs were concerned, and that all I had to do was to switch on the charm and I'd have it made.

At the time they arrived, Derwent was just finishing giving Stella my sister a bath and a brush, and was carrying her back to our enclosure when he was stopped by the man, who took Stella and gave her a big hug. This just about gave me heart failure, for as much as I loved Stella I knew instinctively that this family was for me. Quite apart from which, he already had five girls in the family, plus a wife, and really needed a strong male around to balance things out. He had to be convinced.

There was of course a good deal of excitement when they came into our enclosure, and we were all chasing about and giving effusive greetings, and I could see that they were having some difficulty in deciding which one of us should be chosen. I figured that it was probably the dad in the family who was going to make the final decision, so I went and sat myself down, put on my most fetching and appealing look, and literally willed him to look my way. He eventually did, and then squatted down and opened his arms, into which without any hesitation whatsoever I threw myself. I put my paws around his neck and gave him several very wet kisses and whispered in his ear: "Take me and I'll be your best friend for life". I knew all along that he was a push over, and if that didn't work I didn't know what would. Well, needless to say it did. I knew that I had made the right decision, and it was the beginning of a wonderfully understanding and loving relationship, and I can tell you I was one happy dog.

There followed a few formalities; for instance my new master and missus had to shell out some money to Jack, who in return gave them my papers, which had to do with my family background going back all the way to my great grandpa, which I suppose was worth something as it made me a member of the Canadian Kennel Club, although I must admit that I never was much of a club person, and as I said before, wasn't too keen about either being shown for my looks, or pursuing a career as a bird dog.

They were not too sure how I would react to the car ride. I guess they thought that I might get over excited, or be fretting about leaving my brother and sister behind, or being sick on the journey, so Jack gave me a tablet of Gravol to take, to quiet me down. Actually I was pretty excited, but I didn't need any stuff to make me sleepy, so I pretended to take it, but tucked into the side of my cheek, and after we had got going for a few minutes, as discreetly as I could, I got rid of it. Also because they thought I might not travel well, it was decided that Missus should drive, and my new master (I sometimes flatter him by calling him Boss), would sit with me in the back with the kids. We didn't have the station wagon in those days. It was a bit crowded, and I got to sit on Master's lap, so we could have a bit of a cuddle, and I could put my head out of the window and smell all the lovely farm smells as we drove by. The kids too were giving me all kinds of attention and petting, and I really couldn't have asked for much more. I was in heaven, but there was more to come.

My new family lived in a nice house in what I have always considered to be a fairly good neighborhood, surrounded by a huge garden, and would you believe, a swimming pool in the backyard! Of course I couldn't swim yet, but being a water dog, it was only a matter of time before I would give it a try, but realized that once in, getting out of it might be difficult, as it involved climbing a ladder which I wasn't too sure about, but that is another story

I soon got to know my way around the house, and where everybody slept, and most important, where they had their meals, and where the food was kept. After all if I was going to be part of this family, which I undoubtedly was, I had to know what was what.

I spent the rest of that first day sticking pretty close to my master and missus, who spent the afternoon working in the garden with me alongside. Every now and again they would talk to me, and stop to give me a little petting and reassurance, not that I really needed any, because I knew that I had chosen the right family, and when I went to bed that night, with a full tummy and affectionate 'goodnights', I realized that I was a pretty lucky dog.

CHAPTER 2

I t didn't take me long to get used to the routine in my new home, and looking back I didn't have much to complain about – except the cat. Her name was Pebbles, and for some reason, which for the life of me I'll never understand, seemed to take an instant dislike to me, and an unwarranted distrust of my intentions. All I wanted to do was to say hello and have a little sport with her, but by her reactions you would have thought that I was going to tear her apart and eat her for lunch! She took one look at me, her fur stuck up like a hedgehog, she made a very unfriendly spitting noise, and jumped at least three feet straight up in the air, and scrabbled up the nearest wall clinging desperately to the wall paper, which didn't exactly please Missus. I was told in no uncertain terms to leave her alone. Cats are funny animals actually, you never know what they are going to do next, and it took a long time before she accepted me as one of the family, and even then under what I would call rather restricted terms. I really wanted to be friends, but I guess she always rather resented my intrusion into the family, and assuming such an immediate position of prominence, which I suppose rather put her nose out of joint. I mean, I couldn't help being popular could I? It's just the way I am.

The other problem that arose, and which gave rise to some contention among the family, was about the name I was to be given. You see, in my papers, for which they had paid all that money when they got me, I had been registered as Piper, son of Blond Peppi of somewhere or other, and my mother happened to have been registered as Lady Sophie Rendel. (Later on, because of course we are Canadian, we dropped the title, and to her friends, she was simply known as Sophie.) There was quite a bit in there about my grandparents too, which I'll skip, because I really don't want to brag about my background, and it's not really relevant.

Well, nobody liked the name Piper, which is just as well, because I didn't either. One of the girls suggested 'Rajah', while yet another wanted 'Sahib'. Both sounded quite distinguished, but who ever heard of a blond dog like me having a name like that? It seemed to me that someone had been reading too much Rudyard Kipling. Someone else wanted to call me 'Charlie' or 'Fred', which I really didn't like at all—far too commonplace, and I really felt I deserved better. Anyway, following a good deal more discussion, my master came up with a brilliant suggestion. "How about Simba?" he asked. I have to tell you that this was way before they made the movie 'Lion King' and all that, but as most people know, Simba is the African word for lion, who is of course the king of the jungle, and I must say I rather liked the sound of it, and thought it a highly appropriate name for me. After all, I had a nice yellow coat with curly hair, a long tail, eventually I would develop a deep rich bark, I looked a bit like a lion cub, and provided I was safely secluded by the protection afforded by our station wagon, I had the courage and heart of a lion too! So Simba it was, and while far be it for me to boast, I did actually become quite well known in the neighborhood, and established quite a reputation for myself.

I very soon learned that I was special, that I was much loved, and that within reason nothing was too good for me. My master and missus were determined that I was going to be one of the best kept dogs in all Vancouver. They had even got a book about how to rear Golden Retrievers, including what I should be given to eat to make me big and strong and of course handsome. All of which I thoroughly approved of. Would you believe two eggs (lightly poached), with soft toast for breakfast? Bread and warm milk in ample quantities for lunch, and puppy chow with all kinds of delicious leftovers and gravy for supper. I especially liked the gravy. A dog never had it so good!

That book had all sorts of other things in it about how to train dogs and the like, all of which was really common sense. They could have saved their money, and just goes to show how some folk can make a buck by taking advantage of dog lovers, who want to do things by the book.

I used to get a walk with Master every morning before breakfast and before he went to work, and no matter how tired he was, he would always take me out last thing at night. I knew he was just doing it for me, which made it special. He wanted to make sure that I could do my business, as they call it, in complete privacy, which I really appreciated. Besides it was the only times that we males in the family got to be by ourselves together.

On Sundays the whole family used to go for long walks in a place called Lighthouse Park. You just couldn't imagine what a wonderful place this was! It had huge big trees everywhere, with big ferns and all kinds of exciting places for animals of the forest to hide. And the smells! Enough to drive a dog crazy! The other good thing about it was that we were released from that damned leash, and were allowed to run free and explore where we liked. I used to chase those little squirrels until I was ready to drop! And then of course there was the beach, which was where I first learned to swim. The kids used to delight in throwing sticks far out into the ocean, which I would swim out and fetch, but never give up, as the fun was really the tug of war that followed when they got hold of the other end! This used to make the master as mad as you know what, because I was supposed to be a retriever, but as I explained to you before, in spite of my distinguished ancestry, it seems that I was a bit short on those particular genes, because the whole idea of being a fetcher and a dropper never really appealed to me, and I always thought it to be a highly over rated pastime.

The other thing that I really used to enjoy, but which invariably got me into trouble, was the swamp. In the middle of the Park there was a stagnant stream, which had turned into a bog which grew a whole lot of stink cabbages and other interesting things, and was full of the most delicious black mud. When everyone's attention was distracted, and at the right moment, I would sneak off and plunge myself into this gorgeous morass, and indulge myself in its distinctive and simply divine odours, and would emerge a lovely chocolate colour. What with that, and the scent I had acquired, I felt sure that I would be absolutely irresistible to every female dog in town. Yes, it is quite true that I developed a rather precocious interest in the members of the opposite sex at quite a tender age. I could never really understand why it was that Master got as mad as you know what when I went through these preparations in the hopes of an amorous adventure or two. In every other way he seemed to have such a good understanding of things to do with dogs and psychology and the like, except when it came to these all important needs, when he just didn't get it. I sometimes wonder how he and Missus managed to have all those kids! Anyway I used to get the most frightful telling off, and would be made to go back into the sea to wash, and get rid of my nice smell. Thereafter no one wanted to sit next to me, or give me a hug, until I got home and had been given a bath, which again was usually accompanied by another scolding from the boss.

Actually he should have been grateful to me, because it was partly because of all this that we eventually bought the station wagon. This was much nicer for me, because I had my own area and seat at the back, with a window to allow me to look out. We didn't get the wailing complaints from the girls about my drooling in their hair, except that is when I really wanted to bug them, when I could put my head over the back seat and slobber very effectively! Sometimes I didn't get the respect and consideration I felt to be my due from some of the girls, and I found this to be a great way to get my own back!

I really felt good about being a member of this lovely family, and every thing went perfectly for the first few days. It was a two way street, because I had overheard Master and Missus saying what a wonderfully good dog I was. It had been all of four days since I joined the family, and apart from the odd accidental poop, I hadn't put a foot or a paw wrong. It was on a Wednesday afternoon that I first got myself into real trouble

Master of course went to work every day, and often did not get home until quite late. Missus had to get up terribly early in the morning to get the kids off to school, so she always had a rest upstairs in the afternoon, and I was left on my own which was an awful bore. It's tough being on your own as a puppy. The only person around was the cat, and as I already said, there was no way she was going to play, or even talk to me.

I had been shut up in the kitchen, and the doorway leading into the living room had been shut off by apiece of board, which was all that was preventing me from getting in there. It wasn't too tough to give this a bit of a push with my nose and the whole thing came crashing down, which gave me a real fright I can tell you. Anyway it allowed me into the living room, where it was much more comfortable, and had all sorts of interesting things around.

I got up and stretched myself out on the chesterfield, and rested my head against the arm. It was all very cozy and comfortable, and smelled good. It was then I suppose that I made my mistake. You know how it is with young dogs, especially Retrievers, we like to chew. The arm of the chesterfield was irresistible. I began with just a little nibble, and before I realized fully what I was doing, I had chomped away a good bit of it. I knew Missus probably wouldn't be very pleased about this, so I tried to cover the hole with one of those cushion things. Unfortunately, somehow or another, I got to giving that cushion a jolly good shaking, and before I knew it, the cover was in shreds, and there were little bits of stuffing all over the place! Oh God! I had really done it now. I knew Missus was going to be pretty upset, so I decided that I'd better keep a low profile for the next little while, and put on my most winning ways when she came down. But as you might have guessed, it didn't work. You see it was a brand new chesterfield, and she was really upset with me. I was threatened with being sent back to Langley, and all sorts of other dreadful things, and I got a few sharp whacks with the cane across my butt as well. I didn't mind that so much, but I couldn't have survived being sent back to Langley. I felt really badly; I knew I was in disgrace, and dreaded facing the master when he came home, but made up my mind that I would make the first move, and give him an especially effusive greeting, which would probably soften him up. And then to make matters worse, in my anxiety over the whole thing, I had an accidental poop.

Master was late that night, and as usual rather tired, and arrived home to be greeted at the door by Missus with a scoopful of poop, and "you and your damned dog!" I thought that maybe I should make myself scarce for a while, and hid under one of the beds upstairs, until Master had had his drink and a look at the newspaper. After a while I crept downstairs, and went and put my head on his knee, and told him how really sorry I was, and promised that I would never do anything like that again. He of course forgave me, and I never did do anything like that again- well hardly ever.

Chapter Three

||||||||||||||||||||||||||||||||||||||||||||||||||||||||||||||||||||

As I continued to grow up, life became better and better. Not only did I have a wonderful family, who gave me constant attention and all the affection and care that I could possibly want. I also lived in a very friendly neighborhood, where there were lots of other dog -loving people, who provided me with both extra tidbits of food (which I wasn't supposed to have, but which would have been very impolite to refuse). And of course more attention. Especially from the kids with whom I became quite popular, and were always ready to have a good romp, and with whom I would tag along for the odd unscheduled walk.

One of the things I really liked to do was to sneak behind the kids and follow them to school. It seemed to me that this was a fun place to be, because I got all kinds of attention from the teachers, who kept wondering who I belonged to, and I suppose had some difficulty in deciding which class a smart dog like me would best fit. Unfortunately because I was so popular, it created a bit of a distraction for the children, and all too soon one of my little 'missuses' would let the cat out of the bag by telling everyone who I was, and would then have to phone home with: "Mum, Simba has followed us to school again, and Miss Baynes(the teacher) says you had better come and get him!" Poor Missus would then have to come and pick me up in the car, for which I usually got a jolly good scolding, but being what she was, a real softy, I never took these too seriously, and the extra little outing and the ride in the car made it all worthwhile.

Although I was not permitted to attend the school that the kids went to, I wouldn't want you to think that I wasn't educated, because I most certainly was. Actually, I had to go through a pretty tough period of educational dog training under none other than my demanding master. Whew! Talk about discipline! Marine Corps Boot Camp was a virtual cinch compared with what I had to undergo. It was all because of that damned book they bought. It gave him all sorts of ideas about how a dog was supposed to conduct himself when both on and off the wretched leash, and how I should show myself off by sitting, standing, pointing, walking to heel and all that stuff, and of course to immediately 'come', regardless of what irresistible smells or other distractions there might happen to be around, which was enough to drive a dog crazy.

To begin with, my boss would coax me along by offering me one of those delicious little treat things whenever I did as I was told, but I'm afraid I rather lost interest when the treats ran out, and found the whole thing a bit of a bore. Sometimes I'd try to change the pace of things a bit by turning around in circles and playing the fool. Well I can tell you that was not a good idea, for I'm afraid the boss took these lessons a great deal more seriously than I did, and any such playful interruptions were met by pretty stern measures which included at the very least a swift clip across the butt with the tail end of that leather leash thing which was the bane of my life. Anyway to pacify him I went along with it all, and eventually I learned that when he snapped his heels together, I was expected to immediately sit at attention half a pace behind his right foot, and stay absolutely still. He really seemed pleased when I did this without a spoken command, and in some way must have appealed to some hidden military instinct of his. He used to show this off to his friends who of course pretended to be impressed, but then would rather spoil it all by asking whether I was a good gun dog.

I of course eventually graduated, and was probably given undeservedly high marks, and completed the curriculum in record time, which between you and me, was almost certainly due to Master getting a bit fed up with the routine, and like Jack before him, was a little disappointed with my attention span, and although not exactly a slow learner, I was never what you might call a really keen student. I much preferred going for walks, exploring, swimming, and just messing about with my friends.

I had no shortage of friends, and in a very short time I got to know all the other dogs in the neighborhood, and actually enjoyed an active and a pretty good social life. I developed a routine, which worked for most mornings. I would wait until the kids had left for school, and Missus would be busy with her housework, then I'd sneak off and meet my friends down the road, and we would take ourselves for a walk, or find somewhere to play. Of course we were not supposed to be out on our own, and always created a bit of a caffuffle when we got home, as there was always a bit of a panic about us being picked up by the Pound, who had some pretty mean tricks when it came to enticing dogs into the back of their big white van, which I'll tell you about later. Anyway the scolding and the risks of being caught all added to the fun.

The O'Sullivans lived across the street, and they had no less than three dogs, so that gives you some idea as to what they were like. They always had treats and goodies around, and all you had to do was to wander over there and look fetching, and one would be rewarded with a delicious morsel. They also tended to over feed their dogs, so there were frequently leftovers lying around from which I benefited.

As I said they had three dogs. Two were Spaniels of one sort or another with long floppy ears, which used to droop into their food, so they tended to smell a bit, and they both had bad breath, which rather put me off. One was called Punch, while the other, (a she dog who had been neutered), had the unlikely name of Princess. The third one was a tiny little runt of a thing, who had traveled all the way from Mexico; his name was Pedro, and although he didn't look like a regular breed he claimed to be a Chewawa (I'm not sure how you spell that, but that's how it sounds). I got to be quite fond of him, which I'm sorry to say was always wrongly interpreted by my master. I don't know how he could have thought such a thing, for quite apart from his

20

miniscule size, he walked on three legs, with a funny limp, due to a previous accident when he suffered a bad break which had never been fixed. He also had a rather annoying, yappy little bark. The truth is I always felt a bit sorry for him, because none of the other dogs took much notice of him and he rather got left out of things. Anyway, none of them presented what you might call a threat, and that's one of the reasons why I selected a very large heather bush that grew in their garden, behind which I used to do my business, as they call it, every morning. I can tell you, it grew to be the best looking heather bush in the whole of West Vancouver!

There were about six other dogs that lived down the street, but my best friend by far was a big brown dog whose mother was said to have been a Chocolate Labrador. I don't mean real chocolate, but chocolate colored. His father was of much more dubious origin, and probably the less said the better, for it was always thought that it was he from whom Frank, (that was my friend's name,) had inherited all those bad habits, which from time to time would get me into so much trouble.

Frank was a great wanderer, and as we grew up we had a great time exploring together and there wasn't a nook or cranny in the neighborhood that we didn't know about. He was also, I guess like his dad, very keen on the ladies, and there wasn't a she dog around that we were not familiar with. I hope you've noticed that in dog language, we never ever use the other word for she dogs that some people seem to enjoy using for describing both she dogs, and on occasion even people. We try to avoid it if possible, as it is considered rather bad form. Anyway Frank taught me all about girls or she dogs if you prefer it. And I must admit that although that got me into all sorts of trouble from the master, who as I told you before didn't seem to have much understanding on these matters, it was well worth every bit of it.

It was Frank who got me into trouble with the Pound, who I mentioned before had some very mean tactics to coax dogs into that big white van that they used to drive around in.

One day, I was sitting on the front of our driveway, minding my own business, when who should drive up but the big white van. The driver leans out of the window, starts befriending me, and offers me a cookie. Well you know how dogs are about cookies. Naturally I accepted, and before you could say 'Simba the lion,' they had me in that van, and off to the pound I went. I was pretty upset I can tell you. I mean it was like being arrested and thrown in jail, as if I was some stray dog, and thrown in there with all the real criminal types. It was so degrading! I was also worried that Missus would not know what had happened to me, or where to find me. I needn't have worried, because pretty soon that nasty guy who had fooled me with the cookie, had got the number on my collar and was on the phone to Missus to come and get me, and telling her to bring big bucks to get me out. I didn't like the sound of that too much, as I knew it would mean real trouble, but at the most it would probably mean a pretty severe scolding, and being confined to the end of a leash for the rest of the day, which was certainly an improvement on being in this really horrible place, and keeping such company.

I guess this was partly my fault for accepting that damned cookie from a complete stranger, but the second time I got caught was really all because of Frank's insatiable appetite for the she dogs, and all the hidden pleasures they could provide, in which he had instructed me so carefully.

As every one knows there are certain times when she dogs especially need to have a male dog around. They have special and quite secret ways of putting this about, which is of course a very tempting and quite an irresistible invitation to any self respecting male dog. But would you believe that those Pound people could be mean enough to use this gift of nature to their advantage? Well I can tell you they certainly can and they do.

It all happened on a lovely spring day. I was feeling particularly good that morning as I strutted down the street to meet Frank. We were just exchanging our usual greetings, when who should role up but that damned white van with the little crest on the door, so you know where it's from. And running right behind it was a whole bunch of our friends in the neighborhood who had caught the scent, and who were all wildly excited. Just as they passed us the van stopped, and the driver jumped out and opened the rear door. And what do you know, there in the back were two of the best looking she dogs you ever laid eyes on! (Well I thought so anyway), and as every one knows, when nature calls or opportunity knocks, you've just got to go! There was in fact a mad scramble as to who could be first to get in, and there was absolutely no thought given as to the possible consequences that might follow; I mean this was even worth going to jail for! Which is of course exactly what happened, and although I hate to disappoint you, I won't go into the details of what happened while we were on the way getting there.

Well by this time most of us knew the routine. You know the collar inspection, the phone call, the fines, the punishment, and the whole dismal story. The problem was that because this was the second time they had nabbed me, the fine was going to be a lot heavier. I had been branded as a second offender. This was serious, and to make matters worse, I knew that Master was home, that he had picked up the call, and that he would be coming to collect me. Oh God! I just knew it was going to be a really bad scene. In the mean time that damned cookie man was smirking all over, and telling his friend that it was 'Revenue' day. For two pins I could have got my teeth into his you know whats, and told him a thing or two as well..

My predictions regarding the boss were of course correct in every detail and then some. On occasions like this he was known to have a pretty short fuse, and this was no exception. I had always thought that he lacked understanding regarding my attraction to the ladies or she dogs, but on this occasion I was really proud of him. He had to pay a hefty fine of course, which he reluctantly handed over, but he gave that cookie man a proper telling off, I can tell you, and gave him quite a lecture about the legality of driving around with a she dog in heat (whatever that means), in the back of his van.

Well, it was a pretty tense journey home. I knew he was really mad because he wouldn't even speak to me, and although that didn't last long, I was confined to barracks as they say, for the duration. What was even worse there was talk of building a fence around an area in the back garden, which sounded to me akin to another jail. It was all that damned Frank's fault!

Sure enough, that very next weekend, the boss went out and brought back a whole bunch of lumber and some very ominous looking rolls of that heavy duty fencing wire. I sat and watched as this serious looking bit of construction took place. I did not like what I saw at all, or the fact that he kept muttering under his breath 'this will fix your business', or 'stop you laughing in church' (one of his favorite expressions), or words to that effect.

When it was finally finished, and it took the whole weekend to do it, he had effectively fenced in an area at the back of the pool deck. This was bounded at the back by a wooden fence, one side by the pool shed, the other by a thick hedge, and the front by this horrible looking heavy duty wire fence, which made me feel I was looking out from the wrong side of a concentration camp. This was to be my playpen. Actually it took me right back to those early days in the school at Langley, where there really wasn't much play to speak of, compared with my recent freedom. To be honest I thought Master had taken this whole Pound episode a bit too seriously, and was being rather too hard on me, for although I was now known as a second offender, I had already made up my mind that there was no way that they would ever catch me again.

Well, Monday morning came, (I hate Mondays don't you?), and after my walk and breakfast I was led, and not without a fair amount of protest, was deposited in my pen by Missus. I was pretty sure that if I made enough noise yapping and barking, (I found the yapping particularly effective), that in respect for the neighbors, she would soften and let me out. But not a bit of it, she took no notice and I was left to my own devices.

Well, pretty soon I got tired of the yapping routine, and it was obvious that I was going to have to change my tactics. First I tried charging the fence and trying to scramble up it, but soon found that when the boss builds something, it is built for keeps. It was solid; it wouldn't budge, and was far too high to jump over. So I got to really thinking about it. What was it that those guys in the prison camps used to do to escape? Why, they tunneled. Of course! Why hadn't I thought of that right away? The obvious place to begin was the hedge, as it was the only spot without a concrete foundation. It was a very thick cedar hedge, but after about two hours digging, and I'm afraid not without considerable damage to the hedge, I had burrowed my way through to the next door neighbour's garden, and was free!

With all this exertion, I was not only very hot, but I was also very dirty, and just dying for a swim to cool off and clean up. I had mentioned before that swimming alone in our pool was a bit tricky because of the ladder situation, which I soon learned I could not manage without the help of Master to push me up. But Mrs Wilson who lived two doors down the road had a lovely pool, with proper steps to get in and out, where I used to swim quite regularly. Sometimes by invitation, sometimes not, so I headed over there and had a nice relaxing bath, and then went to look for my friends.

I was having such a good time that I'd forgotten how late it was, and it was well after tea time before I returned home. Oh boy did I get it! I had to hear how Missus had been out looking everywhere for me (including the Pound), and the kids had been out searching the whole neighbourhood and were all upset, and of course they had found that great big hole in the hedge which had been the cause of complaints from Mr Weeks next door, and Mrs Wilson, who was really awfully nice, and a real dog lover, had complained about all the dirt I had left in her pool! There was just no end to it, and worst of all the wrath of Master was yet to come! Oh God! Langley here I come! Altogether it was not a good day. If only he hadn't built that darned fence.

I won't dwell on what transpired that night, as it was not particularly pleasant, and I'd rather forget it. Quite apart from the dressing down I got, I really felt badly about all the wasted effort that Master had expended on my behalf, but probably from all that was said, I didn't feel nearly as badly as he did!

CHAPTER FOUR
||||||||||||||||||||||||||||||||||||||||||||||||||||||||||

About five or six months after I had settled into my new family there was a sudden change, which was one I shall never forget.

I had noted that there was a great sense of expectancy about the house and that preparations were being made for something, but I wasn't sure quite what. Missus seemed to be very excited and happy about something; she seemed to be out shopping more than usual, which was fine with me, as I always got to go along to keep her company and to guard the car, and of course inspect and sniff the groceries. These times however she seemed to be spending hours in places like dress shops, and when we got home she would go upstairs to try things on, and then she would carefully pack them away in one of those suitcase things, which was a strange thing to do with new clothes.

Master too, seemed to be busier than ever, chasing around completing jobs that he had to do, like there was no tomorrow. Life in fact was one long rush, with not much time for walks and the more important things in a dog's life, and I kept trying to tell him to cool it, and slow down, for this sort of hectic pace was no good for either of us, especially for me.

Then one day, it was a Sunday I think, things seemed to be getting back to normal, for Master and I set out for a drive in the car, and we seemed to be heading out into the country. Well, I have a pretty good sense of direction, and before long I realized that we were heading East, and I became increasingly uneasy when I began to pick up the never to be forgotten farm smells, which got stronger and stronger, as we headed east, and then to my utter horror I realized where we were going. Oh my God! We were going back to Langley! Had I done something terribly wrong? I didn't think so. Well, not recently anyway, and I just could not understand why we should be going back to that school, with all its discipline, and having to cow tow to Major and all that. I knew how much my master really loved me. How could he possibly want to leave me here?

My worst fears were confirmed. We arrived, to be greeted by the usual loud barking from all the dogs. There were quite a few new additions since I had last been there, and they were downright cheeky to me, making the most awful suggestions about my being brought back, and not being wanted. This of course was all in dog language that Master did not understand, and could not defend. Then to make matters worse Major came out. He never said a word. He just looked me up and down as if to say: 'Well I told you you'd never come to anything. I knew right from the start when you tore up one of my straw birds that you'd come to no good!' He just gave a great sniff, and showing not the slightest interest, turned around and walked away. I was feeling pretty low I can tell you.

Then Jack came out. At least he remembered me, and gave me a bit of petting to try to reassure me. I could see that poor Master was also having a pretty bad time of it too. He put me on the leash, gave me a big hug and told me to be a good boy. And then Jack started to lead me away. Well I just about went crazy. I couldn't bear to see my master and best friend walking away and leaving me in this awful place. How could he? I just did not understand, and was dreadfully upset. I just about choked myself to death pulling on my leash, trying to get away and back into the car. I'm afraid I put up the most awful noise crying and begging him to come back. It was the worst time in my whole life. Casey came to try to comfort me, but it was no good, and finally I was led back to my old cage where I was locked in, and where I continued to cry for a long time.

Dinner time came. Just a dish of dry dog food; no gravy, and none of the nice leftovers that I had become used to. I wasn't hungry anyway, so you can just imagine how upset I was. I missed my family, especially my littlest 'missus', who used to lean over her highchair and feed me part of her dinner. But most of all I missed Master and Missus. With all that packing and preparation, did it mean they were going away? Were they coming back? And When?... if ever?

I didn't sleep much that night and began to chew my paw, which after a while developed a nasty red, raw spot, which took a long time to eventually heal up, so you can tell how upset I was.

The next few days were terrible. I missed my family dreadfully, and I just could not believe that they would leave me here indefinitely, but when would they ever come and get me out? The worst part of it was that I couldn't figure out why they had brought me here. I knew that I had been pretty much of a trial at times, but they had such a good understanding of dogs, and that we simply can not be good all the time, and that they loved me enough to eventually forgive me for almost anything.

Well the days wore on, each one longer than the last, and even Casey couldn't get me out of my despondency. I think Jack was getting quite concerned about me, for he gave me a fair bit of attention, but he wasn't like my master, and it just wasn't the same. Anyway, one day he told Derwent to give me a bath and a brush and to get me looking my best. Obviously something was brewing, and I soon learned from the other dogs that I was going to be shown at the local dog show that afternoon, and rumor had it that Jack thought that I might be up for a prize, or a 'ribbon', as they call it, which would of course have brought a bit of credit to Jack. But to be honest I didn't see that it would do too much for me, and I didn't feel like being paraded around the place on the end of a leash, and doing all that sitting and standing business, especially in front of all those strangers. I was not a happy camper, and made up my mind right there that I was not going to co-operate, and that once again I would play dumb, so as not to impress the judges. They could keep their Blue Ribbons for all I cared. I just wanted to go home.

Well, we finally arrived at the place where they were having the dog show. Jack had brought two or three other dogs along, all of whom had been in shows like this before. All the way there in the truck they kept telling me what I had to do in the dog ring, and how I had to behave, until I got thoroughly fed up with the whole thing. They were so darned superior about it all, and by the time we got there I was ready to have a jolly good fight if they said another word!

I had to sit on the end of a leash for what seemed like hours waiting my turn to be 'shown'. Each dog had a number pinned on to his collar, to identify who they were, and each in turn was led out into the ring when they had to go through their little performance in front of the judges, who would then walk around and inspect us as if we were some sort of produce to be bought or sold in the market place. The whole performance was quite boring, and to my mind a bit infra dig, and not at all what being a dog was all about.

I did not like the idea of being identified by a number. To begin with, I had what I thought was a perfectly good and most appropriate name. I didn't see why I should be referred to as 'number twenty- one. So I spent a good deal of the waiting time trying to get that number off my collar, and although I wasn't totally successful, by the time I was through it was pretty dirty, and so was I, from rubbing myself on the ground.

There wasn't time to get me all cleaned up again, and poor Jack had to take me into the ring looking quite disheveled, and not at all like a prize winner. In addition to which, to show my disapproval, I put on my most reluctant look and hang dog expression, and pretended not to understand what I was told to do. The Judges frowned their disapproval, but they did agree that in spite of my demeanor, that I was in fact a handsome dog. Jack was busy trying to point out my best features, when I went and lifted my leg against the Judge's table. Well, that did it! The crowd found it amusing, but the Judges certainly didn't, and poor Jack was told in no uncertain terms to immediately remove me from the ring. Without my being awarded even a single mark,

I was led away by an acutely embarrassed Jack amid a titter of laughter from the crowd of onlookers.

As I said before, I never liked the idea of being a show dog. Although I felt rather sorry for Jack, who was really a very nice man, he should not have tried to show me off when I was at such a low ebb, and without the permission of my family. Anyway, I was now in absolute disgrace. None of the other dogs would have anything to do with me, except to say that they were going to report me to Major as soon as we got back to the farm. I just couldn't wait to hear what he was going to have to say, but I really didn't care, for all I wanted was to go back home. I was, as you may have guessed, a pretty miserable dog.

Two or three days went by. I continued to feel pretty miserable, and then quite early in the morning Derwent came to fetch me, gave me a bath and a brushing, and went through the routine which I recognized as a prelude to something special that was going to happen. I began to panic. Oh my God, I thought, they're going to send me away to another home! I just couldn't bear the thought of such an idea, and began to pull desperately on my lead, and was doing everything I could to tell them that there was no way I would have anything to do with that, and that I simply would not co-operate, when all of a sudden, out of the corner of my eye, I got a glimpse of a blue car coming up the driveway. The door opened, and there was my master looking tanned and fit, and he was walking towards me! Derwent released my leash and I bounded forward and leapt into my master's arms, and just about licked him to pieces! Poor Master, I think he felt pretty guilty when he saw my chewed paw, and I had obviously lost a fair amount of weight with all the fretting I had been doing. As for me, I was so excited I just didn't know what to do with myself except to make a bee-line for the car, where I entrenched myself on the back seat, and there was nothing, but nothing, that was going to make me move!

After Master settled up with Jack—(would you believe that he actually had to pay money to put me through all that misery?), and I had said a few rude farewell words to Major, we finally got going. Once we were clear of the gate, I jumped into the front seat and snuggled up to my master who I think was as pleased to see me as I was him, and he promised me right there that he would never ever again leave me in a kennel, and he never did.

It was just so wonderful to be home again. The family made a great fuss of me, and gave me all the attention I had missed so much, and even the cat, in her own superior way, seemed quite pleased to see me.

I eventually got used to the fact that Master and Missus, from time to time, needed to go away on holidays, and that Master was required on occasion to attend conferences, (well, that's what he said anyway), when I was left at home to look after the family, a responsibility that I took very seriously, but I never forgot those three weeks I spent in the kennels.

CHAPTER FIVE
IIIIIIIIIIIIIIIIIIIIIIIIIIIIIIIIIIIIIIIIIIIIIIIII

A few months later, my pleasant routine at home was broken, by a big decision that was made at about this time by my master and missus. I had overheard them talking about the possibility of taking the family (including me), on a camping trip to the wilderness areas of Vancouver Island. I liked the sound of the wilderness, because my friend Frank (the chocolate Lab I told you about), had told me all about his trip up to the lakes, where his master went shooting, and he used to do the retrieving thing and bring back the birds. But in addition to the birds there were all kinds of exciting things going on, with enough new smells to drive you crazy!

I wasn't really sure what camping was all about, but I had caught word about them renting one of those big camper trucks, which sounded like a whole lot of fun, as it would give people like me a lot more room to move around and relax during the journey, for often in the blue car I had to sit on someone's lap, which wasn't all that comfortable, and the kids would always be complaining that I was hogging the seat. I always liked to sit with my head sticking out of the window, so I could catch all the lovely smells, and feel the wind rushing past my ears and ruffling my hair, and of course everyone that we passed thought what a handsome dog I was, which is always good for the ego.

Actually this got me into real trouble one day, because with all this admiration going on, I just leaned a little too far out of the window, and as we rounded a corner, I lost my balance, and fell right out of the car. I banged my head on the road, which just about knocked me out, and I nearly got run over by an oncoming car, which scared me to death and left me quite dazed. Master, (he's a doctor you know), said I was concussed, whatever that means. Poor Master and Missus got a terrible fright too, and from thereon in I had to sit in the middle, and was threatened with being secured by a seat belt, which wasn't really necessary, as one of my little missuses used to hang on to my collar, which at times would just about choke me to death. As a result I couldn't enjoy the smells nearly as well, and of course I didn't get admired as much by the folks on the road and in the passing cars.

Well you can imagine the excitement when Master arrived one evening and parked this huge camper truck in the driveway, and we began to get ready for our holiday, loading it up with all sorts of those suitcase things, and groceries, and inflatable boats and stuff for this camping business. You name it we had it.

The truck was huge. It had a big seat in front, and behind it was like a small house, with seats and a table, but not much room for a dog to move around in. But would you believe? There was an upstairs observation lounge, where you could sit high up and watch the world pass you by! Actually, once we got moving I didn't like it at all. I was scared it was going to topple over every time we went round a corner, in addition to which the floor, (where I had to sit), was very slippery, and every time we went round a bend, I would desperately try to cling on with my claws, and with a horrible scratching sound, I would slide from one side to the other, which would make all the girls laugh at me, but which I didn't find amusing at all. I did eventually have to make my complaints known, and after the first stop I got to ride on the front seat between Master and Missus, which is of course where I should have been in the first place.

That was the first time I ever went on the ferry, which was terribly boring, as I got left by myself in the truck, while everybody else went upstairs, where dogs are not allowed. Ever. Except if you are a blind dog. I don't mean actually blind, but your master or missus is blind, and you are acting as a guide dog, which sounds like a lot of responsibility, and pretty hard work to me, for you have to train for about two years, pass all sorts of difficult tests, and be totally dedicated. I think I'd rather be just a family pooch.

Anyway, we finally, after what seemed like hours, got off the ferry, and started driving again, and after a long time finally reached a place called Englishman's River, where it was clear that we were going to stop for a while, as Master said it was a good place to camp. You just couldn't believe what a lovely place this was! We were in the middle of a forest, with all kinds of exciting trails and smells, and there was a big river to swim in, with lots of pools and waterfalls, which I wasted no time in trying, and for the first time discovered the pleasure in coasting down the river with the current. I nearly got swept away down a waterfall, which seemed to attract a good deal of attention, and every one said what a good swimmer I was. Well, of course I was! I am after all a retriever! (Even if I don't retrieve very well).

After my swim, I returned to the family, who were by this time getting quite worried as to where I had got to, and were all terribly busy setting up those shelters they call tents.

There were two tents, which were like proper little houses, where my little missuses I discovered, were to sleep. They had set out their beds on the ground, and quite forgetting that I was all wet, I went and lay down on one of them to have myself a little rest. Well, of course that got me a proper telling off, and had I taken it seriously, could have ruined my whole day! As it was, Master came to the rescue, and after drying me off, said it was their fault for leaving the tent flap open.

That night the kids slept in the tents, I got to sleep in the back of the camper truck, next to my master and missus, and after a big dinner, I went to bed thinking that holidays and camping were just grand.

Family holidays were always special. This was of course partly because everyone was more or less in an everlasting good mood, and both Master and Missus had more time to devote to the family and especially to me. I have to admit, I just love getting all the attention that I possibly can, (providing its favorable of course), and quite early on I discovered all sort of ways and means of attracting attention and affection, although I'm sad to say, my motives were sometimes misunderstood.

After a day or so, it was decided that we should journey on, so that we could get to the real wilderness that I had heard them talking about. We were going to drive to a place called Beaver Cove where we were going to have to get another long ferry ride to the tip of Vancouver Island where we were going to find the wilderness. Well, we had a very long drive, and we were all getting a bit restless and tired, and when we eventually arrived at Beaver Cove, it was to find that we were supposed to have booked a reservation on the ferry. They had not told my master that it only went twice a week. There was already a big line up, but the Ferryman told us that if we waited, we would probably get on. Well we waited…it was a very hot day. We were all very thirsty, and everyone began to get a bit crotchety, and all my little missuses were complaining about my drooling. Well, you know how it is with us dogs, when we get overheated, that's about the only way we can cool off. We have to do a bit of the panting stuff, and of course you drool in the process!

Would you believe that we had to wait in that ferry line up for over five hours?…And would you believe that we were the very last truck that didn't get on? I can tell you my master was not a happy camper! The air, as they say, went a bit blue, and he had some very choice things to say about the ferry service! I made myself scarce in the back of the truck, and sat very quietly, as I didn't feel any contribution I could make would be particularly welcome, and knew that given a little time he would come around to his normal holiday self, and would accept that we were going to have to change our plans. Which is of course what we had to do.

We turned the big camper truck around and headed back the way we had come, for it was after all, the only way that we could go.

After another long drive, and a lot of discussion with Missus, it was eventually decided that we would go to Strathcona Park.

(Missus always comes up with good ideas in a crisis). It wasn't exactly the wilderness, but it was on the edge of a big lake, and I thought it was a pretty nice place to have a holiday. So it was there that the family put up their tent houses, and I got to sleep in the camper with Master and Missus again.

Of course there was swimming in the lake, and long walks, and rides in the rubber boat with my little missuses, which I wasn't very sure about as it was a pretty bumpy ride, but I went along with it, as dogs are supposed to like going in boats. But to tell you the truth boats and I never did really get along all that well together. I used to get quite nervous when they went too far out from the shore, for I didn't think that particular boat was all that safe, especially when the water got all bumpy and rough.

The best part about this holiday business was that Master and Missus were always in a good mood. We did a lot of exploring in the camper, and what I liked best was in the evenings after everyone had had supper, Master would light a camp fire and we'd have toasted marshmallows....Oh yum! How I loved those marshmallows! One of my little missuses would toast one on a stick for me, and the first time I tried one, I of course couldn't wait to get it off the stick, and didn't realize how hot it was. I got a nasty burn on my lower lip, which left a horrid pink scar, which rather spoiled my smile. One lives and learns, and after that they used to give me mine after it had been allowed to cool. The waiting was awful, and used to make me drool something fearsome!

Then the girls used to entertain Master and Missus around the campfire, when they would act little plays and sing songs. I really liked the songs. They used to sing the Beatle songs, like 'Penny Lane' and 'Yesterday', and there was a lot of laughter, and every one had a good time, including me, and they were what my master used to call 'halcyon days', whatever that means.

Well, this holiday finally had to come to an end. Everyone seemed to be having such a good time it seemed silly to have to go back to the work routine, but Master being what he was, had certain responsibilities to fulfill, which he seemed to take very seriously, and there was nothing for it but to head back home. Which is what we did, and I'm sorry to say that I sulked the whole way back.

However, it's always nice to get home. As soon as they opened the car door I would bolt down the street to find Frank and all my other friends. I just couldn't wait to tell them about all the places we had been, and what a marvelous time I'd had, and to ask in a slightly superior way as to how their holidays had gone, which in retrospect was a bit mean, because I knew full well that they hadn't had one.

CHAPTER SIX
||||||||||||||||||||||||||||||||||||||||||||||||||

It wasn't until some days afterwards that I discovered that not everyone had thought it an ideal holiday, because I happened to overhear a conversation between Master and Missus, when Master expressed the opinion that he'd got a bit fed up with looking for good places to camp, and that he really didn't like driving that huge camper truck, and didn't really feel it was his style, whatever that may have meant.

I guess he was still mad about that ferry business, and not being able to get to the wilderness like he'd promised us. Anyway I heard rumblings about the idea of having a cottage, a small place, perhaps by the sea somewhere, where we could go for our holidays, which would be suitable for the family, and of course for me. Well, this sounded like a pretty good idea, and Missus seemed to think so too, but a week or two went by, and I didn't hear any more, and to tell the truth I sort of forgot about it. Maybe they had just been dreaming about having somewhere like that to go to. I mean, we are all entitled to dream a bit, aren't we?

Well, as I said, I didn't think too much more about it, for I was busy with my routine with my friends and so on, but after about a month had passed, there was a sudden sense of excitement in the house, and at supper time on a Friday evening, it was announced by Master, that on the following day, the family were to go on an outing on the ferry to Vancouver Island. And that they were going to be accompanied by a real estate lady, who was going to show us some property!

Well this certainly created a lot of excitement I can tell you!

Everyone started to talk at once, with all sorts of questions that of course Master couldn't answer, and he finally had to tell everyone to 'cool it', for we were only just going to look. I of course knew better, for it was just like when they went to 'look at the puppies', right?

I just couldn't wait to go on another trip. Although I must say, I wasn't all that keen on another ferry ride, for its such a long time to be on your own with nothing to do, and such a temptation not to have a little chew at the car upholstery, or to explore the groceries, or the lunch basket that they would always take along on these occasions from which emanated such divine smells. And of course there was no way one could have a pee or anything like that. One just had to hold it.

I was really looking forward to this family outing. So you can imagine my disappointment when on the following morning, a rather fat real estate lady wearing a blond wig and those great big round glasses, which were in fashion at the time, arrived in a big shiny new car. It turned out that one of the 'come ons' to clinch a sale, was that she was going to transport the family to look at all these properties, and that dogs were definitely not included in the agenda. So that gives you an idea of what sort of person she was, and I just hoped that my master wasn't going to get sucked into some deal, which wouldn't meet with my approval.

Well, to cut a long story short, it was decided that I would have to spend the day with the Eckfords next door.

I always really liked Mr Eckford. He had a way with dogs, and you could tell right away that he liked us. I used to go across the way and give him a greeting whenever he came home, which I think made Master quite jealous, but because I was so friendly, they often used to give me delicious little leftovers from their dinner, which of course wasn't very good for my figure, but which would have been very bad manners for me to refuse. I really liked Mrs Eckford too, but I had had one or two unfortunate misunderstandings with her in the past, concerning the matter of food.

What happened was this. On one particular occasion she had

put a big bowl of soup out on the back porch to cool. And part of my routine in the mornings was to check out the neighbours back yards, so naturally when I saw it set out on the deck I assumed it had been put out especially for me, so I gratefully slurped it all up! It was jolly tasty too!

Another time she was having guests in for dinner, and she had covered a large steak with some liquid stuff, and set it out on a small table on the back porch. I couldn't believe how lucky I was to have such generous neighbours, and of course I ate the whole thing! It was only after I had wolfed the last morsel that I realized that I had obviously made a serious mistake, for she suddenly appeared and there was a great wail of: "Simba!" It turned out that that the steak wasn't meant for me at all, but for her dinner guests, who were due to arrive in half an hour.

But how was I to know? I am sad to say that this misunderstanding was a cause of some serious embarrassment for Missus and Master, and for a while I was in really big trouble I can tell you.

Mrs Eckford, being the nice lady that she was, and being a great friend of my missus, of course eventually forgave me, but I'm afraid she never ever put anything out on the back porch again!

But to get back to the Real Estate saga. The family were very late in coming home, and because I had been left behind and was feeling quite left out of things, I pretended not to be too enthusiastic about welcoming them home, and put on a bit of a sulk, which didn't last very long, especially after I had been given an extra nice dinner, and had heard the news.

It turned out that they had all had a very tiring day with lots of ferry rides, and that the fat lady (with the blond wig and the frog eye glasses), had taken them around to a number of properties, and tried to talk them into the benefits of each one, but Master, and especially Missus, who is very smart in these matters, weren't having any of it.

All of these properties were located on an island called Gabriola, and in order to get there, would you believe? You have to take yet another ferry. I didn't like the sound of that too much, because I've already told you how I feel about ferries, but from everything Master had said, it sounded as if all this journeying might be worth it.

They also had a bit of a laugh about the fat lady. Apparently, while they were exploring one of the properties she had to show them, she snagged her blond wig on a tree branch, and the wig went tumbling down a precipice, and Master had to risk his neck to go down and retrieve it. This was all sort of embarrassing for her, as her proper hair, which was gray, and quite wispy, wasn't nearly as nice! Anyway it serves her right, for if she had taken me along, I could have retrieved it without any fuss for her...but then perhaps I might not!

It seems that the fat lady saved the best for the last, for right at the end of the day she took them to see this place which was at the far end of the island. This was apparently quite a large property being much bigger than they had anticipated buying, and with a price tag that was much higher than they could afford. The truth was however that it seems that Master just fell in love with it on sight, and was convinced that somehow this was a very special place, which was just meant for a family like us, and was determined that we would find a way to eventually have it. It was situated right on the ocean with a lovely sandstone beach, with woods at the back and a nice sunny grass meadow in the front above the beach. It had acres of Park on one side of it, and more woods and a farm on the other, so there was all kinds of room and space to have our privacy, which is what my master really liked. Not that he was anti- social or anything like that, but as I said, he didn't care too much about camping right next door to people that he didn't know, and putting up with all their noise and behaving in ways that we as a family were not accustomed to. I mean we all have to have a little peace now and then, don't we?

Well, the outcome of all this was, that he let it be known to the fat lady that he was very interested in the property, and while we couldn't afford to buy it outright for ourselves, he thought that he could interest some of his friends to buy it jointly, and that we would then divide it up. So he talked to the man who was selling the property, (he didn't like dogs, and I didn't like him), and it was agreed that Master would return with some friends in one week to have another look at it, and see what could be arranged.

Well, the whole of that week everyone, especially my master, seemed terribly pre- occupied with this property business. They seemed to talk about nothing else, to the extent that I didn't get nearly as much attention as I had become accustomed to, and even my walks were curtailed. Master was forever on the phone talking up his friends about buying a share in this wonderful property that he had found. They really seemed to have been smitten by this cabin fever thing in a big way, and by the end of the week he had persuaded three or four of his friends to rent a small airplane for the day, and to fly over to Gabriola to inspect the property for themselves. Which is what they did.

There apparently was a lot of discussion and negotiation both between his doctor friends as to who were interested and who wasn't, and with the man who was selling the property (who didn't like dogs), who wanted to enforce certain conditions into the deal, which some of them weren't entirely happy about.

Well, eventually after what I thought to be a lot of shilly-shallying, the deal finally went through, and my master, together with two of his friends, became the owners of this wonderful place. I knew all along that somehow Master would manage to swing it, and that's how I got to meet and become friends with the Litherland and the Cookson families, and soon discovered that they too were doggie people. Well they would have to be wouldn't they?

The Litherland's dog was quite old. His name was Robbie, and although he wasn't what you might call a purebred, (he was part Beagle and part Labrador I think), he was really nice. It was agreed that we would be friends, but at the same time we would respect one another's property boundaries and family rights.

The Cookson family had a dog called Rusty, so you can figure out what color he was can't you? He was a lot younger, so it was expected that he should treat both Robbie and me with due respect, which he did, and we all became good pals. It was agreed that we would never eat each others food, that we would observe the boundaries that we had marked out in the traditional way, and that we would not go into each others houses without being invited in, and encroach on any family affections. In short, that we would be good neighbours. And we were. (Well, most of the time.)

Of course these families had kids too, and as they were all much of an age, they would join together in all sorts of activities in which we often took part, we all had great fun, and life was wonderful.

I'll never forget our first holiday on Gabriola. Of course there was no cottage to begin with, for it took a year or two before that was really completed. There was a lot of bush and several big trees that had to be cleared before they could build, so to begin with we used to camp, and that was really great. I loved camping. We had three tents, two for my little missuses, and of course I got to sleep with Master and Missus. Well, for the first night that is. The first night we arrived we were all very tired, what with the travelling on all those ferries, and all the work setting up camp, so Master just pitched the one big tent and we all went to bed together. Of course what they hadn't reckoned on was that I had never been exposed to all those irresistible smells of the deer and raccoons and the other creatures of the forest that come out at night. I simply had to get out and see for myself what was going on, and as this happened every few minutes, I suppose it must have disturbed everyone. But then I was there to protect them wasn't I? In addition to that, it had been terribly hot. To cool off, I had of course been doing a lot of in and out of the water, and was bringing a lot of unwelcome wet into the tent. Also I had not yet learned that it was not a good idea to drink sea water, and was being sick all over everyone in the tent. By the time morning came I was really feeling awful. As you know, Master is also a doctor. He was very concerned about me, for in the morning I looked pretty sick, and there was some talk of having to take me home to the pet hospital. Master said I was suffering from severe electrolyte imbalance, dehydration, and hyperkalemia, whatever that means. Anyway I was put to bed and given lots of water and juices to drink and after a few hours was able to stagger about again, but it took a few days for me to feel my normal self. After that I learned never to drink sea water again.

So I came in for a good bit of scolding I can tell you, and from there on I was put to sleep in the back of the big blue car, which actually was a pretty good deal for me, as I had the whole back seat to myself where I could stretch myself out, but I didn't like the idea of not being able to get out when I wanted to...or needed to, and of course could not conduct my guard duties like I was supposed to.

Actually I thought that sleeping on the back seat was such a good idea, that when we got home, and it was time to go to bed, I made straight for the car, but was told in no uncertain terms that that arrangement was strictly for holidays only. Too bad really, because you see I never really had a proper bed of my own at home. I used to sleep most of the time in the back hall near the door, not just to guard the place, but because there was a nice cool draft that came under the door. In the morning, when Master got up to make the tea, I would always go upstairs with him, and join him and Missus in their bed, where we would say our good mornings, after which I would feign a very deep sleep with heavy breathing. But unfortunately this didn't fool them for a minute, and I had to get out when they got up, and I was not allowed at other times. I really liked their bed, it was sooo comfortable!

But to return to our holidays. That first holiday, we had a lot of rain, which was a pretty good test as to whether the family was really going to enjoy it there. Master had rigged up a big plastic sheet so we could do our outdoor cooking out of the rain, and he'd even built a rack for all the dishes, and shelves to store the food. Well, those shelves and dishes got me into one big fight

I can tell you. It happened like this. On about the second day after we had settled into our camp, we had a visit from Dr. Tyhurst, who was the man who owned all that big piece of property next door to us. Actually he was a nice man, who really liked dogs, so he had to be nice right? Anyway he had two dogs. One was just a small dog; he was a Cairn, called Sandy. The other dog was a much larger one. He was a Basset hound, and his name was Quintus. Well, Quintus was a pretty nosy dog. From the start, I felt that he was not properly respecting what was our property. He gave the impression that he was boss everywhere, and before you knew it, he invaded our kitchen, was sniffing around our dishes, which was bad enough, but when he lifted his leg and peed all over them, that was just too much! So I really went after him. I got him by the scruff of the neck, and was giving him a really good shake and a telling off, when who should come from behind and grab hold of my tail, but that little runt Sandy! That really hurt, because you know how sensitive dogs are right there, and that really made me mad! In the meantime Dr Tyhurst and Master were trying to be polite to each other, for after all, they were now neighbours, and it was a social call, but which finished up by them both having to separate us.

We both got a proper telling off. But I realized afterwards, it was put on just as a show of politeness, for I was, after all, protecting our property and had every right to go after him, and although we were always civil to each other subsequently, we never became what you might call good friends.

In the following year it was decided that the family would build a cottage, which was really good news, for obviously it was the intent that we should be spending our holidays there, which was absolutely fine by me, for I could think of no place else that I would rather have been. It had everything that a dog could possibly want. In fact I couldn't understand why we just didn't move lock stock and barrel over from Vancouver and live here permanently. But then of course that would have interrupted Master's work...and every one has to make a living, especially if you are going to have all those children AND a dog! All of which requires big bucks.

So the building of our log cabin gradually progressed. Actually what happened was, that the other two families decided to build at the same time, about which they were all very chuffed, because they were able to get a special 'deal', and my master is what you might call a real sucker for a deal. Well, the deal was not without some problems, for first of all we had a whole pile of carpenters and other workers who descended on the property, who camped with their families on the property that just about drove me mad. They were what you might call 'itinerant workers', were non union, and they took their time, so instead of the building being finished by the school holidays, as promised, it took the entire summer, and during pretty well the whole of it, they had a jolly good holiday on our property, and made a proper nuisance of themselves. This was the down side to the 'deal'.

The other problem was that the families were all vying with each other to see who could get their cottage finished first, for the 'deal' was so good, that everyone was worrying about the builder going bust.... which he eventually did, but luckily not before the buildings were completed. And wouldn't you know it? We were the very last to get the roof on, and to have it finally finished, at the very end of the summer, or early fall.

Well, it was all worth it in the end, for this was just my sort of place, with not too much fancy stuff lying around to get me into trouble, and there was a lovely big fireplace to toast myself at when I came in all wet from swimming, which of course used to get Missus in a snit, and poor Master would have to go and dry me off, and I suppose being what you might call a frequent swimmer this became rather tiresome for them, but I just couldn't resist it, for after all I was born to be a water dog!

The only problem with all that swimming was that I used to get a really sore crotch, which had to have cold cream put on it every night. That was OK in the summer when it was really hot, but in the winter it felt pretty chilly, and I wasn't keen at all ...well you know how sensitive that area is... and he used to have to chase me, which of course was another way of getting attention.

We didn't just go to the cottage in the summer either, for that year we spent a whole week between Christmas (I love Christmas!), and New Year. It snowed and snowed until it was about a foot deep and I had a great time romping about in it with my little missuses.

I must admit though that I got a bit scared when they put me on that toboggan thing and we went careering down the hill and almost into the sea, the edge of which was all covered with ice and was so slippy that I had trouble getting out, and that made everyone laugh at me, which I didn't think was funny at all.

The other thing I liked with the snow was that it made it so easy to pick up the trails of all the little creatures that live in the forest. There were zillions of them, which kept me busy all day. It was much easier to spot the deer that I loved to chase, but could never catch up with. (My master says it's very bad to end a sentence with a preposition, but don't you think 'up with which I could never catch' sounds sort of silly? I do.)

Talking of chasing things, there were one or two other situations that really used to excite me, and usually happened when we were walking along the beach. There were a couple of old Blue Herons that used to stand on the edge of the water on a point. They would stand perfectly still, first on one foot and then on the other, looking into the water to catch a glimpse of the small fish, who would be pushing their luck by swimming around at the edge of the shore. Following a quick lunge, they would end up being gulped down for supper. Those Herons were so intent on this that I never thought they would be able to see me sneaking up on them. But do you know that just as I was getting within reach of grabbing that long feathery tail, they would invariably lazily flop their great wings, and with a loud squawk of derision, would slowly take off. I never was able to catch one, and they used to drive me mad!

The other creatures that really used to bug me were the Otters. There were lots of them about, and whenever they saw me taking a stroll along the beach, they would swim in towards the shore, and poke their little heads up and taunt me to come in after them. As I told you already, I am a very good swimmer, so I would take a running dive and swim out to where they were waiting for me, but just as I got up to them, they would bob down and disappear. This was very confusing and also very temper trying, for while I was desperately trying to locate them, they would suddenly pop up a few yards away, and laugh at me. And to make matters worse Master and Missus would laugh at me too. Talk about frustration! I often used to dream about catching these little rascals, but they were just too quick for me.

Christmas was an especially nice time in our family. First of all everyone seemed to be in an everlasting good mood. Master was home for most of the time, and we all got presents.…. that is except for the first year. I had been sent outside to do my business as they will call it, and then I happened to look through the ground floor window, and there they all were exchanging presents. I just about went berserk! I couldn't believe that they would leave me out of all the festivities, and that they hadn't even got one present for me! I just about broke the window trying to get in! Anyway Missus soon got the message, and one of the children wrapped up a rag doll in pretty paper and gave it to me, which I pretended to be a surprise, and with much feigned excitement tore off the paper (the best part), and with a big smile on my face, and a lot of tail wagging, I took it round to show everyone, and then to vent my spleen as they say, I gave it a jolly good chew. Later that evening they made up for their little faux pas by giving me an extra helping of leftovers, including a helping of Turkey and all the trimmings, including the stuffing,.(I just adore stuffing!). They never forgot to buy me presents again, or to leave me out of any of the family festivities. After all I was an important member of the family, as other than Master, I was the only male!

The next summer was even better, because Missus took me with all the children to live in the cottage for almost all the summer holidays. Master would come over after work at the weekends, and we just had an idyllic time. There was always something going on. We had lots of walks, swimming whenever I liked, playing with the family or the other dogs, and fishing and boating. I really wasn't too keen on either of these two last pursuits, even although my master tried very hard to encourage it, for he really liked to have my company. I only went fishing once, and rather disgraced myself. Master caught a huge salmon, which was jumping about in the boat, so of course I pounced on it, and in doing so, just about capsized the boat, and of course in the process, that damned salmon slipped over the side and got clean away! I tell you I was in BIG trouble! I never heard such language, and I was not invited to go again. I didn't really care one way or the other actually, because if there are no fish being caught, just sitting in a boat is deadly boring, and a bit much to expect from a dog. Furthermore, I didn't like the way the boat wiggled about, and I was afraid of falling off into the middle of the ocean, (even though I am an excellent swimmer.) The other thing I didn't like about it was the noise of the engine, which hurt my ears.

I am sorry to be going on about how good I am at swimming. I know it sounds rather immodest, but my master says that nowadays the psychologists are telling every one that they shouldn't be shy about saying how good they are at things. It's supposed to project a positive image of yourself, and give you confidence. And contrary to what our forebears may have taught us about modesty being a virtue, too much of it can give a person an inferiority complex. And I certainly wouldn't want to be saddled with that. Ever!

The other reason for not liking fishing was that on one occasion I got well and truly hooked. The children used to go fishing off the rocks. They had a long stick with a string attached, at the end of which there was a very nasty hook thing that they used to bait with bacon to attract the fish. The trouble was that they would forget to take the bait off the hook, and would leave their fishing poles on the verandah. Well, have you ever heard of a dog that could resist bacon? I bet you haven't. Anyway the long and the short of it was that I couldn't resist nibbling away at that bacon, and of course got the nasty sharp hook stuck in my lip, you know, the thick leathery bit. Master says it's called the cartilage, whatever that is. Well, as you can imagine this really hurt, and I was having a terrible time trying to get it out. Fortunately Doctor Master was home, and so was the other doctor neighbour Doctor Litherland, and they had a consultation as to what they should do. Clearly the hook had to be removed. Dr Litherland, who was actually a chest doctor, declared that this was a job for a surgeon, which is of course where my master came in. Trouble was that he didn't have any of his fancy instruments with him, nor did they have any anaesthetic to dull the pain. So after further consultation with Missus, (who as I said earlier is always good in a crisis), it was decided that Doctor Litherland would sit on my head, that Missus would sit on my body, and that Master would operate. Which he did, with a very large pair of pliers, which I didn't like the look of at all! Naturally when I saw what was about to happen, I struggled like mad, but with all that weight on me there really wasn't much I could do, and in the end Master was very quick. He pushed the sharp barbed end of the hook through my lip, and then with the pliers cut off the sharp end, and then pulled it out. What a relief! I was really grateful for what they had done, in spite of the lack of anaesthetic! Doctor Litherland said I should be given a medal, but I got a candy instead, which was OK by me. So you can't blame me for not liking fishing can you?

As I mentioned once before, the one thing I lacked at home was my own bed. I could never understand why I wasn't designated one, for anyone who knows anything about dogs knows that we have to have a place that we can really call our own, where one can hide, quietly snooze, sulk, or sometimes simply just ruminate. Well for some reason, perhaps because I was just too big, and a proper bed would have taken up too much room. It would have created a bit of a clutter in the house. (Missus can't stand clutter! Everything in the house has to be as neat as a polished pin, so you can imagine the fuss over a few wet paw marks!) So the long and the short of it was that I just had to make do. As I told you already, at the house I used to sleep at the back door where there was a nice cool draft, but at the cottage it was a bit better. I'd lie in front of the fire in the winter, which was nice and cozy, but after everyone went to bed I'd sneak up and settle myself on the chesterfield.

In the summer it used to get terribly hot. Can you imagine going to bed in the summer dressed in a heavy overcoat? Well, I can tell you it's not much fun, which is one of the problems of being a water dog and having a thick silky coat. I looked everywhere to find a nice cool place which had a soothing cool draft, but there simply wasn't one, until one particularly hot night I found the answer. Why, the bath of course! So when everyone had done their various jobs in the bathroom and retired to bed, as quietly as possible, I'd climb into the empty bathtub, which was deliciously cool, and I'd sleep like a top, (if tops really sleep).

The family got quite used to this, but when we had guests, and they got up to go to the loo at night, they'd have a fit, and on more than one occasion they awoke the household by yelling: "The dog's drowned in the bath!" To which my master would patiently explain: "It's alright, Simba always sleeps there in the summer", and everyone one would then go back to bed.

Another time, my master took me over to the cottage with just one of the kids - no Missus - they hadn't had a tiff or anything like that- well, I didn't think they had, but anyway, he had come over to do some project or other, (which were everlasting, and took up a lot of dog time). Well, I realized that without Missus he would be pretty lonely in bed, so before it was really bedtime, I quietly sneaked in and tucked myself in on the side of the bed that Missus always slept on. Don't you think that was thoughtful of me? I do so love my master, and do so like to be near him. Well when he found me there, I think he was quite touched, and he gave me a big hug, and told me it was a nice try, but that it wasn't going to work! He said it very nicely of course, but my feelings were really hurt. You can but try, can't you? So off I went back to the bath. Ugh!

CHAPTER SEVEN

W ell, the years seemed to pass by very swiftly. They do when you're having fun, don't they? Sometimes though, the days themselves can go terribly slowly. Especially Mondays. As I already told you, I hate Mondays, (except when we are on holidays).

Before you would know it, my little missuses were growing up. First the boy friends started turning up, and then the weddings started happening. I wasn't at all keen about those. The tarrydiddle and preparation that went on in connection with all this was unbelievable. Missus was in a snit for weeks before hand. Master was chasing around getting the garden all tiddly, and when he wasn't doing that, he was off working...I guess he was in a panic about all the big bucks he was having to spend... and as a result there wasn't much time for walks, or for dogs for that matter, and to tell you the truth I felt a bit neglected, and couldn't wait to have it all over.

I never did like the entertaining thing. I don't particularly like crowds of people in our house, for they are all too busy socializing to take any notice of me, and I generally feel quite left out of things. And seldom do I ever get any of all the delicious goodies that they usually have to eat on these occasions, which they keep passing around, and make me all drooly at the mouth.

I remember the first big party they had after I joined the family. You never saw so many people in your life all squished into our living room, all standing around eating and drinking, making a terrible noise, and there literally wasn't enough room for a dog to go and lie down. I was getting more and more fed up...

have you noticed that one becomes more impatient as you get older? I have. Anyway it was getting very late. It was past everyone's bedtime, including mine, and it was time they all went home. So to show my displeasure, and to give them the message, I did what I suppose was a rather rude thing to do, (and after the telling off that I got, would never do again), but I went and lifted a leg against one of the living room chairs and let off a few squirts.

Well! This certainly got their attention! One of the guests stood there, and with an accusing finger pointing right at me yelled: "Look at the dog! Look at the dog!" And before you knew it I was the center of attention! I got a terrible tongue lashing from the missus, but it was worth it, for not long afterwards everyone went home.

There weren't many things I didn't like about our house, but parties were one of them. The other thing I didn't like was when those long ski things appeared in the back hall. There was a pair of funny looking yellow boots, (can you imagine my master in yellow boots?), and a pair of sharp poles that went along with them, and when these appeared I knew he would be gone for the whole day. There was no way that I was going to get to go with him. I never said good-bye on those occasions, and would put on a jolly good sulk to show my disapproval.

Later on in his career, a bag of golf sticks used to appear in the back hall, and I got to learn that that was bad news too.

The other thing I didn't like were carrots. I used to shove these on the side of my dish, which was sometimes a bit of a problem, for with only a nose and a tongue, it was hard to do without leaving some other tasty morsel behind. Missus continued to feed me these nasty orange leftovers (my missus never wastes ANYTHING), and I suspect these were shoved onto my dish, because there was someone else in the family that didn't like them either.

After that first wedding, life was never quite the same. I felt I was losing some of my joie de vie. I had put on too much weight, and I noticed that I was getting very gray around the snout. I was getting a terrible aching feeling in my hips when I walked, and Master said I had arthritis...I guess all that swimming in freezing cold water didn't help. I was spending a lot of time just sleeping, and I noticed that I was having to pee all the time, and sometimes I couldn't hold it at night, which was pretty awful, but my master was very understanding, and never scolded me for it, for he knew I couldn't help it.

I was also having a terrible time with gas. My master says as you get older, you don't digest your food as well, especially meat (and I love meat). He says the bacterial flora (whatever that is), changes, and as a result, you form a lot of gas in your insides. And this used to get me into quite a lot of trouble. Well, you know how it is. When you get a bit distended in certain places, you just have to let it off, don't you? And so that no one would know who it was, I would of course try to let these discreet little puffs off very carefully and quietly, but I'm afraid I couldn't do much about the smells. Phew! I must admit that sometimes they were pretty bad, and would immediately invoke the ire of my little missuses, who would complain: "Dad! Simba's smelling up the house again!"

I'm not sure what they expected poor Master to do about it, but if I did it too often, I'd get sent outside. It was all so embarrassing! Getting old is hell isn't it?

The trouble with young people is, that they don't understand about getting old do they?

When you're young, you think you're going to stay young forever and ever don't you? But you're not, because as you get older, all these awful things start happening to you, and before you know it, you're like me. So there we are. But sadly their turn will eventually come too, but for their sake, I hope it won't come too soon.

I do so wish I were young again.

And then my second little missus got married. It was another big wedding, and all the preparations that went along with it.

I really wasn't feeling at all well. I wasn't enjoying my walks anymore. It was a real effort to walk up the hills. Also a lot of my friends in the neighbourhood had gone to the happy hunting grounds as they call it, and I figured that my turn would not be too long in coming.

Master took me on my last trip to the cottage, and I guess he knew things were pretty far-gone because I wasn't interested in swimming any more.

Anyway, I made it through my second little missus' wedding, which was a very big occasion, and just a bit too much for me.

I awoke in the morning with a terrible pain in my chest, feeling quite breathless, and was unable to get up. Master found me in the early morning, when as usual he came down to make the tea. He at once realized that I was pretty sick. He listened to my chest with his stethoscope, and I heard him say to Missus:" Simba's fibrillating,"(whatever that means), but I reckoned it wasn't good, for then he said:

"I think he's had a heart attack".

He looked at me very lovingly and said: "It's time, isn't it old friend", and gave me a big long hug. I knew just what he meant, and was very happy to trust him to do what we both knew to be right.

They gently picked me up and placed me on a blanket in the back of the car, and we slowly drove to the Pet Hospital, where they were expecting me. Master carried me into the back office where there was a couch where they laid me down. My doctor Vet was there, who was very kind and gentle. Master held my paw while they shaved it, and then they gave me a needle, which didn't hurt at all. My master gave me a last hug, and then quite peacefully, I went to sleep.

EPILOGUE
||||||||||||||||||||||||||||||||||||||

Life was never quite the same after Simba left us. We all missed him most dreadfully. The house seemed awfully quiet without his effusive early morning greeting, and again, when any of us returned from being out, for even only a brief while. Most of all though, we missed him at our cottage on Gabriola Island, which was his own very special place. But this was where a part of him will always remain for us, and where at times by some strange power, we could sense his presence. As we drove through the woods along the familiar winding makeshift road, with its moss covered rocks and glades of ferns, we were sure that he was there, bounding along, leaping over the fallen trees and brush, with his ears and beautiful blond feathers of his tail streaming behind him, nose to the ground, in pursuit of some real, or sometimes imaginary, quarry.

I would sometimes sit on the bench overlooking one of my favourite views across the strait to Breakwater Island, as we often used to do together, just enjoying the beauty and peace of this wonderful gift of nature. On these revisitations I could all but feel his warmth, as he snuggled up against me. Physical contact and touching were always so important to him, which was after all, both his assurance of my deep affection for him, and his own particular way of expressing his love, as only animals can do.

A year or two had passed, when for a variety of reasons, we for a time, inherited two dogs to look after, that belonged to two other members of our family. One was a Golden Labrador named Chiot, (which in case you didn't know, is the French for puppy), the other was a spunky little Cairn called Benji, who under circumstances of disapproval, would answer to Benjamin.

These two, like David and Jonathan, were bosom friends. They did everything together, and were in fact inseparable.

Strangely, after they joined us, we were never quite as certain or aware of Simba's ethereal presence. Perhaps the void created by his absence had been partly, but never completely filled. Maybe we had, as they say, 'adjusted' to living without him.

Chiot and Benji eventually were returned to their rightful owners, and they too, have sadly, now passed through the gates that lead to the Happy Hunting grounds.

It was a year or two later, that quite by chance that our daughter Judy, (Simba's number three 'little missus'), happened to catch sight of an advertisement in the local newspaper, which was looking for a home for a Golden Retriever.

The story went something like this. The breeder had had this dog returned to him by the owners. They had had him for almost a year. They were both out working full time. The poor dog was shut up in the house all day by himself, so it is little wonder that the destruction level was pretty high. The owners, who obviously were not 'doggie' people, became very upset. There was no improvement with punishment, and eventually they took the dog, who had been given the name 'Murphy', to a vet, with the request… would you believe? …to have him put down.

The Vet naturally was very upset that such a thought had ever arisen, and informed the couple to return the dog to the breeder from whom he had been purchased.

The breeder was now advertising for a home for Murphy. But let's get this straight. Prospective buyers were going to have to pass some fairly vigorous testing to qualify.

Well, to cut a long story short, it had a very happy ending, for naturally they fell in love with Murphy, and Murphy with them. He had, as they say, fallen with his 'bum in the butter', and could not have been luckier had he won the Lottery!

By coincidence Judy and her husband David had bought the house from us when we vacated it. It was of course the house where Simba had lived such a happy life. And Murphy was now inheriting all it had to offer, along with three 'little missuses'.

There was much excitement when they were elected as the new owners of this lovely dog, and I was immediately informed of the new arrival, and hastily went to pay my respects to the new addition to the family.

The greeting I received was really quite remarkable. Murphy came bounding out. There was much wagging of the tail, huge smiles, and several licks ensued. And then he grabbed hold of my sleeve and began to 'talk', which continued on for about five minutes. He still does this every time he greets me, and as far as I know, other than his 'Granny', who is also occasionally honoured in a similar manner, I am the only one for whom this special greeting is reserved.

He is a beautiful dog. Similar to Simba in every way, but is if anything a little more obedient!

What he is trying to say to me of course, when he talks is:

"Don't you recognize me? Can't you tell? I'm back!"

Do you know, I do believe he's right! Anyway, I rather like to think so.